# There Must Be Magic

First Poems for Children

# There Must Be

♛ HALLMARK CHILDREN'S EDITIONS

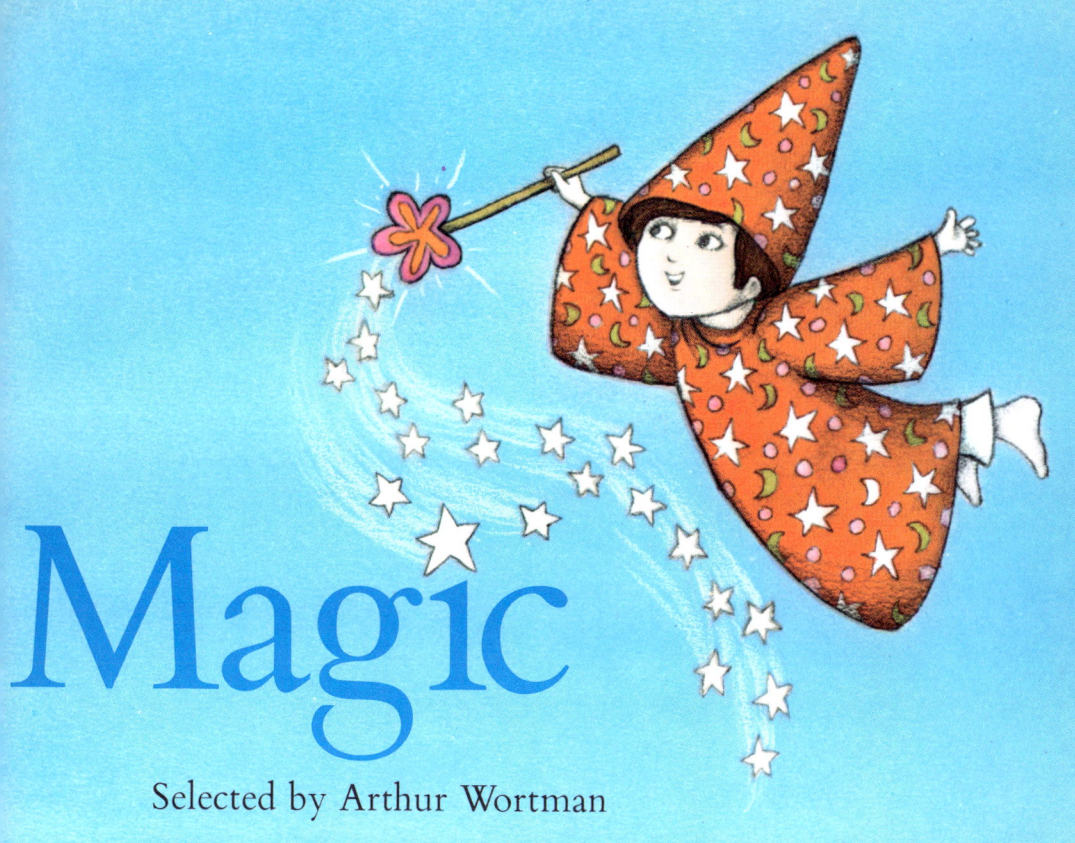

# Magic

Selected by Arthur Wortman

Illustrated by John Overmyer

"Mud" by Polly Chase Boyden, from *Child Life* Magazine, Copyright 1930, 58 by Rand McNally & Co. "First Snow" from *A Pocketful of Rhymes* by Marie Louise Allen. Copyright 1939 Harper & Brothers. Reprinted with permission of Harper & Row, Publishers. "What They are For" reprinted by permission of G. P. Putman's Sons from *Here, There and Everywhere* by Dorothy Aldis. Copyright 1927, 28 by Dorothy Aldis; renewed 1955, 56 by Dorothy Aldis. "I Have to Have It" reprinted by permission of G. P. Putnam's Sons from *All Together* by Dorothy Aldis. Copyright 1925, 26, 27, 28, 34, 39, 52 by Dorothy Aldis. "The Little Turtle" reprinted with permission of The Macmillan Co. from *Collected Poems* by Vachel Lindsay. Copyright 1920 by The Macmillan Co., renewed 1948 by Elizabeth C. Lindsay. "The Day Before April" by Mary Carolyn Davies from *Child Life* Magazine. Permission granted by Georgia Warm Springs Foundation. "Otherwise" from *Up the Windy Hill,* by Aileen Fisher. Reprinted by permission of Scott, Foresman and Company. "Dogs" Copyright 1946 by Marchette Chute. From the book *Around and About* by Marchette Chute. Published 1957 by E.P. Dutton & Co. Inc. and reprinted with their permission. Designed by William Gilmore.

Copyright © 1970 by Hallmark Cards, Inc. Kansas City, Missouri. All Rights Reserved. Printed in the United States of America. Library of Congress Catalog Card Number: 77-102160. Standard Book Number: 87529-055-8.

## CONTENTS

Otherwise · *Aileen Fisher*
What They Are For · *Dorothy Aldis*
Mud · *Polly Chase Boyden*
Whisky Frisky · *Anonymous*
The Day Before April · *Mary Carolyn Davies*
Singing · *Robert Louis Stevenson*
I Have To Have It · *Dorothy Aldis*
The Little Turtle · *Vachel Lindsay*
Eensy Weensy Spider · *Anonymous*
Extremes · *Anonymous*
Dogs · *Marchette Chute*
First Snow · *Mary Louise Allen*
Twinkle, Twinkle, Little Star · *Jane Taylor*
Happy Thought · *Robert Louis Stevenson*

# OTHERWISE

There must be magic,
Otherwise,
How could day turn to night,

And how could sailboats,
Otherwise,
Go sailing out of sight,

And how could peanuts,
Otherwise,
Be covered up so tight?

# WHAT THEY ARE FOR

Curbstones are to balance on
Far from the ground,
Railings are to slide upon
And trees for running round.

Fences are for wriggling through,
Cracks and holes to hop,
And, though she does not like us to,
Puddles are to
    *Plop.*

# MUD

Mud is very nice to feel
All squishy-squash between the toes!
I'd rather wade in wiggly mud
Than smell a yellow rose.

Nobody else but the rosebush knows
How nice mud feels
Between the toes.

## WHISKY FRISKY

Whisky Frisky, hippity-hop
Up he goes to the treetop!

Whirly, twirly, round and round,
Down he scampers to the ground.

Furly, curly, what a tail!
Tall as a feather, broad as a sail!

Where's his supper? In the shell.
Snappity, crackity, out it fell.

# SINGING

Of speckled eggs the birdie sings
And nests among the trees;
The sailor sings of ropes and things
In ships upon the seas.

The children sing in far Japan,
The children sing in Spain;
The organ with the organ man
Is singing in the rain.

## I HAVE TO HAVE IT

I need a little stick when I
Go walking up the street,
To poke in cracks as I go by
Or point at birds up in the sky
Or whack at trees we meet.

I need a stick to zim along
The fences that we pass;
I need a stick for dragging through
The gravel or the grass.

My father says there cannot be
A single doubt about it:
I have to have a stick with me.
I cannot walk without it.

# THE LITTLE TURTLE

There was a little turtle.
He lived in a box.
He swam in a puddle.
He climbed on the rocks.

He snapped at a mosquito.
He snapped at a flea.
He snapped at a minnow.
And he snapped at me.

He caught the mosquito,
He caught the flea,
He caught the minnow,
But he didn't catch *Me!*

# EENSY WEENSY SPIDER

The eensy weensy spider
Went up the water-spout.

Down came the rain
And washed the spider out.

Out came the sun
And dried up all the rain,

And the eensy weensy spider
Went up the spout again.

## EXTREMES

A little boy once played so loud
That the thunder, up in a thundercloud,
Said, "Since I can't be heard, why, then
I'll never, never thunder again!"

And a little girl once kept so still
That she heard a fly on the window sill
Whisper and say to a ladybird
"She's the stillest child I ever heard!"

# DOGS

The dogs I know
Have many shapes.
For some are big and tall,
And some are long,
And some are thin,
And some are fat and small.
And some are little bits of fluff
And have no shape at all.

## FIRST SNOW

Snow makes whiteness where it falls.
The bushes look like popcorn balls.
And places where I always play,
Look like somewhere else today.

## TWINKLE, TWINKLE, LITTLE STAR

Twinkle, twinkle, little star,
How I wonder what you are!
Up above the world so high,
Like a diamond in the sky.

# HAPPY THOUGHT

The world is so full of a number of things,
I'm sure we should all be as happy as kings.